FREEDOM'S THUNDERBOLT

Allied Command Europe
Mobile Force (Land)

Carl Schulze

The Crowood Press

Designed by Frank Ainscough
Printed in China

This edition published in
Great Britain 1998 by
The Crowood Press Ltd
Ramsbury, Marlborough
Wiltshire SN8 2HR

A CIP catalogue record for this book is available from the British Library

ISBN 1 86126 183 7

(Front cover)
The AMF(L) badge, officially introduced in 1961, shows two gauntleted hands clasped over a lightning flash and the initials AMF on a green ground. The hands symbolize the co-operation and solidarity of the NATO states; the gauntlets, a military organisation; the lightning flash, the force's mobility and rapid reaction capabilities; the green ground is the colour used by SHAPE, and shows the status of AMF(L) as a unit of Allied Command Europe.

Abbreviations used in text:

ABCT	Airborne Battalion Combat Team
ACE	Allied Command Europe
AMF(L)	Allied Command Europe Mobile Force (Land)
AMF(A)	Allied Command Europe Mobile Force (Air)
ASOC	Air Support Operation Centre
ATOC	Allied Tactical Operation Centre
CINCNORTHWEST	Commander in Chief Allied Forces North-West Europe
CINCSOUTH	Commander in Chief Allied Forces South Europe
COMAMF(L)	Commander AMF(L)
CSS	Combat Service & Support
DDO	Dienstältester Deutscher Offizier (Senior German Officer)
FAA	Forward Administrative Area
FAC	Forward Air Controller
FADE	Force Air Defence Element
FARP	Forward Arming & Refuelling Point
FASC	Force Air Support Centre
FDC	Fire Direction Centre
FEA	Force Engineer Advisor
FHU	Force Helicopter Unit
FLOT	Forward Line of Own Troops
FMA	Force Medical Advisor
FOO	Forward Observation Officer
FSCC	Fire Support Co-ordination Centre
HQ	Headquarters
IALCE	International AirLift Control Element
IRF	Immediate Reaction Force
LSW	Light Support Weapon
MCC	Movement Control Centre
MEF, MEU	Marine Expeditionary Force, Unit
MSR	Main Supply Route
NBC	Nuclear Biological Chemical
NMT	National Movement Team
OAS	Offensive Air Support
OC	Officer in Command
RLC	Royal Logistic Corps
SACEUR	Supreme Allied Commander Europe
SAR	Search And Rescue
SHAPE	Supreme Headquarters Allied Powers Europe
SETAF	Southern European Task Force
SOP	Standing Operational Procedures
TOC	Tactical Operation Centre
UKNLLF	United Kingdom/Netherlands Landing Force
VB	Vorgeschobene(r) Beobachter (see FOO)
VRV	Vordere Rand der Verteidigung (see FLOT)

Author's foreword

The Allied Command Europe Mobile Force (Land) is a topic too complex to cover in comprehensive detail on 64 pages. Moreover, during the time I was researching this book (1992-97) the force was continually restructured and adapted to new security policies in Europe. The contingents of the different nations also changed; units were disbanded and their missions handed over to others - sometimes even to those of another nation. Units associated with the force were sometimes unable to participate in AMF(L) exercises because they were already conducting missions in Somalia, Bosnia, Cambodia or Northern Ireland, their place in the ranks being taken by others. This multitude of changes and adaptations in fact showed the high level of flexibility which is one AMF(L)'s great strengths.

During the production of this book many nations also ran extensive modernisation programmes, often including new uniforms, new NATO-calibre 5.56mm rifles and new vehicles; a photo taken only a couple of years ago can sometimes be of mainly historical interest, but in order to illustrate the great variety of AMF(L) I nevertheless feel it is necessary to include some older pictures. Although this book can only give a limited snapshot of AMF(L) and its units, I hope nevertheless that it offers a firm basis for the interested reader's studies of this important NATO immediate reaction force.

Acknowledgements

First I would like to express my thanks for access and information to the press information officers of AMF(L), without whom this book would not have been possible: Major Oliver, Major Bangham, Major Mieville and Major Hutchinson. My special thanks go to Oberstleutnant Haupt, the senior German officer (DDO), without whose help I would have been unable to visit many exercises in Norway and Turkey; to Lieutenant Colonel Gibbon, Commander Force Artillery AMF(L), who opened many doors for me; and to the members of the "Dinosaur Club", especially to Oberstleutnant Helleland. My gratitude also to: Captain Hegge, Major Leibniz, Major Sigvartsen, Lieutenant Colonel Verhulsdonk, Oberstleutnant Wattke, Hauptmann Ockel, Stabsfeldwebel Stöberlein, Oberstleutnant Leitbrandt, Major Hauss, Leutnant Wittner, Major Bergheim, Captain Armstrong, Oberstleutnant Gerlach and Hauptmann Greipel. I am also grateful to the members of the Forward Repair Group Combat Service & Support Battalion AMF(L), who got my Land Rover back onto the road; and, of course, to all the countless anonymous soldiers who kindly let me take their pictures and answered my questions. Finally, my thanks to Ms Britta Nurmann, without whose help and encouragement this book would never have been written.

Carl Schulze

Allied Command Europe Mobile Force (Land)

The AMF(L) is NATO's only multinational immediate reaction land force which is directly subordinate to the Supreme Allied Commander Europe (SACEUR). Strategically it is a highly mobile, lightly armed unit with the strength of a brigade. It was formed in 1960, by which date NATO analysts had realized that although Central Europe was well protected against aggression by a heavy multinational presence, this was not the case on the northern and southern flanks, where the Warsaw Pact could probably act faster than NATO was capable of reacting. Furthermore, at that time NATO's former doctrine of massive retaliation was being replaced by the more realistic strategy of flexible response, requiring "scaleable crisis management". The mission of the AMF(L) since then has been to show a potential aggressor that an attack against one NATO partner will draw a response by the forces of all NATO nations. Of NATO's 16 member nations the following 14 contribute troops to the force pool of AMF(L):

Belgium (since formation of the force)
Denmark (since 1996)
Germany (since formation)
Greece (since 1996)
Great Britain (since formation)
Italy (since 1963)
Canada (since 1964)
Luxembourg (since 1969)
Netherlands (since 1989)
Norway (since 1995)
Portugal (since 1997)
Spain (since 1992)
Turkey (since 1996)
United States (since formation)

Missions

Despite the dissolution of the Warsaw Pact and the resulting fundamental change in NATO strategy, AMF(L) has retained its important role as NATO's immedite reaction force. Its ability to deploy to any part of the Allied Command Europe (ACE) command area at an early stage of any crisis makes it one of the first assets to be taken into account by NATO's crisis management staff. To ensure this rapid deployment capability AMF(L) is directly subordinate to SACEUR, without any intermediate levels of command. Although NATO has command of other multinational forces - e.g. the Airborne Early Warning Force, Standing Naval Forces Atlantic and Mediterranean, Allied Rapid Reaction Corps, etc. - none of these has AMF(L)'s ability to demonstrate NATO's determination and solidarity by such rapid deployment. The force's main missions are as follows:

To be ready to deploy anywhere within the ACE area; to conduct deterrent operations; if deterrence fails, to conduct combat operations; if the need arises, to conduct humanitarian and

In the heat of Turkish ranges, an observer from 2nd Royal Canadian Horse Artillery sits surrounded by the whole range of FOO team equipment; note GPS receiver in background, and tripod-mounted AN GV-5 laser range-finder.

peace-keeping operations. Effective deterrence demands deployment to the crisis area at the earliest possible moment; AMF(L) is not subject to the normal national or NATO alarm procedures, especially in that it can deploy in times of political tension before any armed conflict arises.

Contingency Areas and Alarm Structures

In its original mission deployment of AMF(L) was only planned for seven so-called contingency areas. These were: northern Norway (the Tromso and Finnmark region); Denmark (the island group around Zeeland as well as Lolland and Falster); northeastern Italy (Yugoslavian border); northern and eastern Greece (Yugoslavian and Bulgarian borders); northern Turkey (Thrace, Bulgarian border); southern Turkey (Turkish-Syrian border); and eastern Turkey (borders with Georgia, Armenia and Iraq). Today's NATO strategy has AMF(L) earmarked for deployment throughout the ACE command area.

A request for deployment can be triggered by a NATO nation which faces a threat; by one of the NATO subordinate commands (CINCSOUTH or CINCNORTHWEST); or by

Allied Command Europe Mobile Force (Land) Force Pool

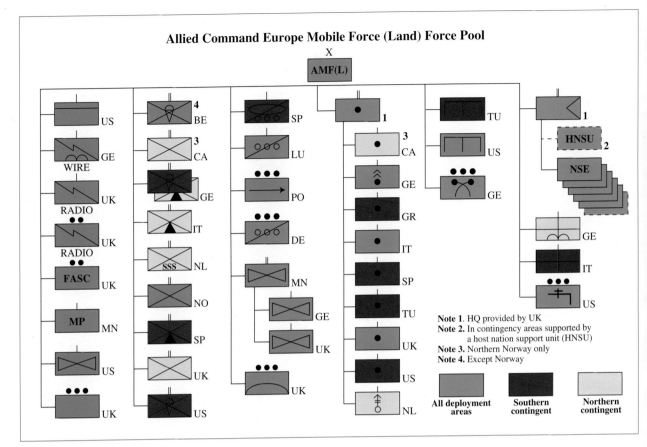

Note 1. HQ provided by UK
Note 2. In contingency areas supported by a host nation support unit (HNSU)
Note 3. Northern Norway only
Note 4. Except Norway

All deployment areas | Southern contingent | Northern contingent

SACEUR himself - the party originating the request would normally consult the other two beforehand. On receiving a request SACEUR presents his military assessment of the situation and a recommendation to the NATO Military Committee, whose chairman then informs the Defence Planning Committee. The members of the DPC inform their respective governments and present their reactions to the DPC. If the DPC now reaches a unanimous decision to commit AMF(L), deployment can begin. SACEUR can bring AMF(L) to a state of immediate readiness at any time during this process. As soon as the units of the contributing nations reach the deployment area they are subordinate to SACEUR only. He can, however, delegate authority to regional commands for deterrence and combat missions, although not below corps level. The COMAMF(L) always maintains tactical control.

HQ AMF(L) and the advance elements - about one third of the whole force - can move into the deployment area on 72 hours' notice, and have another 48 hours to be combat-ready; the air elements of AMF(A) and the most important ground elements have only 48 hours' notice. The rest of the brigade has up to seven days to prepare; another six days are neeeded for deployment, so that within 13 days after the alarm is given the whole force can be in the deployment area. The force pool of units under AMF(L) command numbers over 13,000 men; depending on whether the deployment is to northern or southern Europe ("northern or southern options"), only those force pool units earmarked for this option are chosen to form a 6,500 or 7,000-strong task force. Some nations provide units for the northern or southern options or special deployment areas only.

Multinational HQ

The multinational HQ of AMF(L) is based in Heidelberg in Germany. Apart from the post of COMAMF(L), which is rotated, each post is tied to one nation; nevertheless all elements are structured multinationally. The structure of the HQ follows the NATO system and contains the following elements:

G1: Personnel and payment
G2: Intelligence services, security, and situation of enemy
forces (current and following battle)
G3: Training, command and deployment, planning
(current and following battle)
G4: Logistics and medics
G5: CIMIC (civil/military co-operation)
G6: Signals
PIO: Press information office, subordinate to G1 as
separate cell
G3-Air: Co-ordinates the deployment of helicopters
and other aircraft in the operational area
Force Provost Marshal: Command of the multinational
military police unit, subordinate to G1

HQ AMF(L) is supported during deployment by a US HQ Company of the 3rd Corps (3 COSCOM), which provides tents and vehicles for the HQ, sees to provisions, offers the whole range of administrative support, and on exercises is also in charge of guarding the command posts. (In a real deployment this task would fall to host nation platoons; in both cases part of the job is done by the multinational Force Military Police Unit.)

In the deployment area AMF(L) establishes five command

posts: TOC-Main, TOC-Alternate, TOC-Rear, LOG-Base and FAA. TOC-Main is the command post from which COMAMF(L) controls the operations of his brigade. Similar to HQ AMF(L), it is separated into several cells: G2, G3, G6, FASC, FSCC and FADE. To support the TOC, advisors for engineer missions (FEA) and NBC missions, a CSS representative, a metereological cell and an administrative element are attached to the command post. Usually the TOC is set up so that the cells are literally next door to one another; members of all cells hold a daily O-group together with COMAMF(L) and/or the chief-of-staff.

TOC-Alternate is set up identically to TOC-Main and can take over its functions if TOC-Main is in movement or is non-operational for any other reason (for tactical reasons TOC-Main changes position every 24 hours). LOG-Base, the supply centre of AMF(L), is operated by the HQ company of the British CSS Battalion. FAA is a small, advanced spin-off of LOG-Base.

Co-located with LOG-Base or FAA is TOC-Rear, with cells for G1, G4, G5 and CSS, and a medical advisor (FMA). TOC-Rear is separated from TOC-Main because G1, G4 and CSS are best located near the logistical centre and in close contact with each other; G5 is detached from TOC-Main and TOC-Alternate because its necessary contacts with local civilian authorities might violate military security.

Communications within AMF(L)

As the operational area of AMF(L) can measure 150km by 200km and the command posts are distributed over the whole area, AMF(L) has the following three signal elements:

Luftlandefernmeldekompanie 9 (LLFmKp 9 - Airborne Signal Co.9)

AML(F) units use the BV206 Hägglund over-snow vehicle in many roles, due to its high cross-country capability. The 4.4-ton two-car system has four driven tracks; both cars are steered, steering being transferred hydraulically from the front to the rear car. With a 2.5-ton payload the BV206 can reach 52km/h on roads or packed snow. Here it tows Italian 105mm pack howitzers and carries the crews and ammunition.

249 Signal Squadron
A Troop, 244 Signal Squadron

Apart from connecting the command posts of AMF(L) they also provide telephone connections to the different Force units and to the higher NATO commands. LLFmKp 9 is based at Dillingen, Germany, and is nicknamed "Wire Company"; it provides encrypted telephone lines to the host nation and NATO HQs, sets up links to host nation and NATO telephone networks, operates communications centres, and provides cable connections as well as a radio relay net to connect the command posts. The extensive signal equipment of the company features microwave link equipment FM1000 and FM15000, an MKS switchboard (AUTOKO 90) and, in future, a "BIGSTAF" set which can establish a local wireless telephone net and connect different available nets. It is planned to equip the ten radio relay troops with BV206 tracked vehicles; all the unit's vehicles are already airportable.

Britain's Royal Signals provide 249 Signal Sqn from Bullford; this unit has two satellite communications troops with Skynet 4B VSC501 uplink stations which can establish connections to NATO HQs and other units all over the world. They also operate HF and VHF connections to all AMF(L) combat units with radio sets of the Clansman series (VRC 321 and VRC 322).

To each combat unit they attach two two-man teams with Land Rovers, who train unit personnel how to handle the sets and then establish a 24-hour connection with them. 249 Signal Sqn also establishes and operates two secure - i.e. encrypted - VHF radio nets: the Command Net, connecting all command posts and units, and the Log/Medical Net, connecting the relevant sections of all units. The squadron is also in charge of the Movement Control Net, a teleprinter net which connects LOG-Base, FAA, the airfield and the port.

A Troop of 244 Signal Sqn provides the UHF, VHF and HF ground-to-air net, the connection to AMF(L) and FHU aircraft, and establishes permanent connections to ATOC and ASOC. On all networks established by AMF(L) units the English language is used.

Apart from all these communications networks the computers used in TOCs and LOG-Base also have to be connected; an LAN (local area network) is established in the TOC, also including LOG-Base. The network is connected to NATO's wide area network (WAN), and in future other HQ elements will also be connected.

The command post of AMF(L) can also serve as a divisional command post. If this is required further signals units have to be attached, as seen during exercise "Strong Resolve 95", during which AMF(L) commanded the MEF and UKNLLF in addition to its own units.

Force Military Police Unit

This unit combines elements from all contributing nations: British, American, Norwegian, Danish, Greek and Luxembourg MPs, Belgian Gendarmes, Dutch Marachaussee, German Feldjäger, Italian Carabinieri and Turkish Asiz. The command post is set up by Britain's 158 Provost Co RMP, which also provides a platoon of 17 MPs with NCO rank. In the deployment area the Force Provost Marshal, from HQ AMF(L) in Heidelberg, takes command of the unit. Patrols are usually formed multinationally; the common insignia is a blue brassard or plate with the NATO star and the letters "MP".

The military policemen have a broad variety of tasks. They have to translate all movement orders into action; to reconnoitre and signpost the march routes; and to guide and supervise traffic on these routes. They perform similar duties along the Main Supply Routes (MSR) connecting ports, airheads and railheads with the staging areas and the LOG-Base. The police tasks of the unit comprise enforcing discipline and investigating criminal and traffic offences; whenever possible these investigations are led by the MP unit of the nation to which the concerned soldier belongs. The unit is also in charge of the security of VIPs, and advises G4 in all questions concerning prisoners of war.

Logistical Support

The Combat Service and Support Battalion provides the command post for the logistical apparatus of AMF(L), which controls and supervises the operations of the CSS's different elements (transport company, forward logistic support squadron, supply company, REME workshop, postal and pay service), and co-operation with national support elements. These latter see to the needs of their respective national contingents, and put their different branches under command of the CSS.

All these units are located together in LOG-Base, which can

occupy up to eight square kilometers if ammunition is also stored there. They also operate the FAA together, which is located about 20km behind the front line. The list of supplies which are organized and sent up to the troops includes fuel for vehicles and aircraft, all kinds of provisions and munitions, spares, clothing, detergents and lubricants - virtually everything a soldier might need, down to toilet paper.

The CSS is also in charge of maintenance and repair of vehicles and equipment. An assembly point is set up where vehicles and equipment are dropped off by recovery teams; from here they are sent either to the Forward Repair Group (which is assembled from service units of the different nations and located in the FAA), or to the REME Workshop in the LOG-Base, depending on the difficulty of the repair.

The Host Nation Support Unit, usually of battalion size, supports the CSS Bn in its tasks, especially where transport, acquisition of provisions and other goods, and the provision of heavy engineer machinery is concerned. The HNSU also speeds up the deployment of AMF(L) by helping with the transport of arriving units, and may also provide military police and guard elements.

If deterrence fails...

The deployment of AMF(L) is subject to a special set of rules of engagement covering every eventuality. Rule No.1 has four stages dealing with the deployment of the "key companies"; Rules Nos.2 to 5 deal with the several levels of escalation, from observing and reporting up to shooting back. If the deterrence which is AMF(L)'s primary mission fails, these special rules of engagement are replaced by the regular NATO rules of engagement for armed conflicts.

AMF(L) can be deployed as a regular multinational light

(**Left**) Bell UH-1D of the German Heeresfliegerstaffel 9 lifting an underslung load for a Spanish artillery unit during exercise "Ardent Ground 97" in Turkey. The rigger will move out from underneath towards the right front of the Huey, to avoid the tail rotor as the chopper lifts away.

(**Right**) Royal Netherlands Marine mortarman explains the sights of the British-made L16A1 to a comrade from the US 1/508 Airborne; note the Dutchman's US-style camouflage fatigues, and brassard with national and AMF(L) patches. During cross-training the exchange of personnel such as mortar crews between national units is quite common.

(**Below**) Norway's Telemark Bn, identified by bright green berets, parade during exercise "Strong Resolve 95", which was Norway's AMF(L) debut. Volunteers for this unit must be willing to serve outside Norway, and for a second year on stand-by after completing the normal year's conscript service.

infantry formation under the regional command of the host nation. This is naturally subject to the brigade's capabilities: having no armoured units, and having only short range artillery and anti-aircraft assets, AMF(L) needs support from host nation units which are more fitted for these tasks. Mobility in theatre is also limited to the brigade's own helicopters and vehicles. These seeming disadvantages are balanced by the fact that AMF(L) can be deployed throughout Europe as a multinational unit, and can lead up to six battalion-size battle groups simultaneously. Its light structure is in reality one of its greatest advantages, given the consequent high scale of anti-tank weapons like TOW and Milan, and the capability to conduct missions in difficult terrain. Last but not least, AMF(L) can provide the HQ for a Combined Joint Task Force, and serve as an advance element for other NATO immediate reaction forces such as the ARRC.

(Below & opposite below) Eleven nations contribute up to 17 squadrons and seven AA units to AMF(L)'s air support (previously designated AMF(A), but since 1995 IRF(A) - Immediate Reaction Force/Air - headquartered at Kalkar, Germany). Powerful reconnaissance, air superiority and ground support forces can quickly be formed to counter any particular threat, with a forward command post in the operational area. Typical IRF(A) structures might include, e.g.: one each Belgian and Netherlands F-16 squadrons, an RAF Jaguar squadron, and a US F-15 squadron; or alternatively, e.g.,a Belgian F-16 squadron, one each German and Italian Tornado squadrons, and a US A-10 squadron. Here, an F-16 of the USAF 388th Tac Ftr Wg takes off from a Norwegian base; and one of the RAF's latest Harrier GR7 V/STOL jets, with eight pylons to carry a wide variety of ground attack weapons.

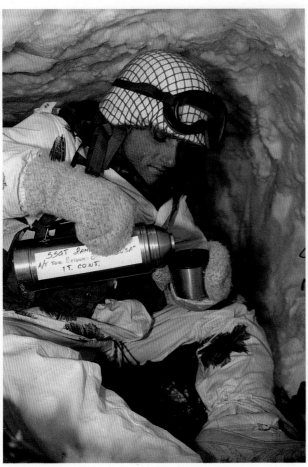

(**Left**) Italian soldier of the AT Ptn, Susa Bn, 3rd Alpini Rgt, having a brew before leaving his snow-hole for duty. He wears a German camouflage suit, Canadian boots, and the "Fritz"-type ballistic helmet which is becoming increasingly widespread in NATO.

(**Opposite top**) Until 1996 the German Luftlandeartilleriebatterie 9 (Abn Arty Bty 9) operated the Italian 105mm pack howitzer under Force Artillery – the only unit with this type in the Bundeswehr, seen here during live firing in Norway.

Heavy Equipment

This list of weapons and equipment is based on an exercise in 1997, during which AMF(L) fielded nine artillery batteries and a mortar battery under its Force Artillery, as well as the mortar companies of the combat battalions, the helicopters of the FHU, and the heavy equipment of the brigade units.

20 helicopters
48 105mm howitzers
8 LARS
12 120mm mortars
16 81mm mortars
24 Stinger ADA
15 TOW
42 Milan
15 Wiesel
8 CVR(T) with 30mm cannon

Deployment

Successful deterrence depends on deploying the troops of AMF(L) to the operational area as quickly as possible. As stated above, given 72 hours' notice HQ AMF(L) and advance elements totalling one third of the force can arrive in the deployment area within 48 hours, the remainder within a further six days. The degree of urgency and the location govern whether the force will deploy by air, sea, rail, or a mixture of all three.

The fastest method is of course by C-130 or C-160 aircraft. For this purpose NATO's International Air Lift Control Element establishes a command centre in the deployment area from which it operates the airhead; transport aircraft land at ten-minute intervals around the clock for six days to bring in the force's personnel, equipment and vehicles. In emergencies IALCE can also call on the huge C-5 Galaxy, C-141 and C-17 Globemaster aircraft of the US Air Mobility Command, and the Airbuses of the Flugbereitschaft der Deutschen Luftwaffe, to carry the heavy equipment; these larger aircraft naturally take more time to turn around.

An example of rail deployment was provided during exercise "Action Express 93" in Denmark when, apart from aircraft and ships, AMF(L) used 32 trains with 20 to 40 wagons each.

From the home country to arrival in the nation of deployment responsibility lies with the National Movement Team (NMT), which co-ordinates freight space and transport to ports, airports and rail stations. After arrival in the deployment country the force's Movement Control Centre (MCC) handles further

(Above) Truck Utility Heavy of 5 (Gibraltar) Fd Bty RA leaves a "Ro-Ro" ferry in a Zeeland port during "Action Express 93"; during lower readiness states civilian and military ships carry equipment to deployment areas while the troops fly in.

(Opposite top) Belgian Para-Commandos unload a train which has brought their vehicles, weapons (including Milan transport cases) and equipment to the deployment area.

(Opposite below left) C-5 Galaxy of US Air Mobility Command (insignia, inset) unloading Bell UH-1H of 6th Aviation Rgt (SETAF).

(Opposite below right) Italian Alpini disembark from a C-130 Hercules during "Arctic Express 94".

deployment; host nation transport is provided for personnel whose own vehicles have not yet arrived. The heart of the MCC is a movement control platoon of Britain's Royal Logistic Corps, reinforced by elements of other nations. As the operation or exercise continues the MCC co-ordinates convoys and the transport of units in co-operation with the FMPU, and of supplies in co-operation with the CSS Battalion.

The "key companies" deploy into their operational areas immediately to begin their deterrence missions. Until their equipment arrives the other newly arrived soldiers stay in the holding area, which usually consists of camps, hangars and barracks close to the airhead. After the heavy equipment arrives the troops are brought to it by host nation transport. From here they head on to the staging area where they wait for their missions. Logistic elements deploy to the LOG-Base.

11

Great Britain

Together with the other three founding nations of AMF(L), Great Britain today provides one of the largest contingents under force command. This comprises, at time of writing:

3rd Battalion, The Parachute Regiment
Headquarters Force Artillery AMF(L)
5 (Gibraltar) Field Battery RA
249 Signal Squadron
244 Signal Squadron
33 Squadron RAF
Combat Service & Support Battalion
84 Intelligence & Security Section
Force Air Support Centre, 1 UK Group, RAF Odiham
Movement Control Platoon, Royal Logistic Corps

The **British AMF(L) infantry battalion** rotates every two years; e.g., 3 Para took over the AMF(L) mission from the 2nd Bn Royal Green Jackets. Other units to fill this slot in the relatively recent past have been 2nd Bn Royal Regiment of Fusiliers, and 1st Bn The Duke of Wellington's Regiment. The British AMF(L) infantry battalion always comprises an HQ and service company, three rifle companies and a combat support company, altogether numbering 679 all ranks.

The three rifle companies each have a command section and three rifle platoons; each platoon consists of three eight-strong rifle sections and a command section. The British infantry section has two LSW and six SA80; for anti-tank purposes there is one LAW80, and at platoon level there is a 51mm smoke and illumination mortar. The eight snipers of the battalion are subordinate to the reconnaissance platoon of the combat support company; they are equipped with the L96A1 rifle. For deployments in northern Norway the infantry use the BV206 Hägglund tracked ATV, otherwise they have Bedford trucks.

The combat support company fields eight Scimitar or Sabre CVR(T) tracked armoured recce vehicles in its reconnaissance platoon; nine 81mm mortars L16A1 in its mortar platoon; six Milan guided anti-tank weapon systems in the anti-tank platoon; and nine GPMG (Sustained Fire) in the machine gun platoon. Elements of the combat support company are often attached to the infantry platoons; and the recce platoon is used as a screening unit in combination with the Milan and GPMG, which are for these purposes mounted on BV206s or Land Rovers.

For AMF(L) command the eight Scimitars are an enhancement to the Luxembourg and Danish recce elements, often doing long range reconnaissance or advance-to-contact work in the operational areas of other AMF(L) components, e.g. working together with German Wiesel vehicles.

84 Intelligence Section is part of HQ AMF(L) stationed at Heidelberg. The section performs all intelligence tasks for AMF(L), working closely with the intelligence services of host nations.

(**Opposite**) In northern Norway the deep snow prevents use of the GPMG on its normal sustained fire tripod mount - it sinks into the snow while firing. Here men of Support Co, 2nd Royal Green Jackets avoid this by using a *pulk* sled, which also simplifies transport - the gun, 50 rounds, and tripod together weigh over 27kg (69lbs). In this role the GPMG can engage targets out to 1,800m.

(**Above**) 2RGJ sniper using the 7.62mm L96A1 Accuracy rifle; with Schmidt & Bender 6x42 optical combat sight, and special ammunition manufactured to very low tolerances, effective range is up to 1,000m. Because of the very low temperatures in Norway snipers have to undergo special training to enable them to stay inside their hides for long periods without being discovered.

(**Right**) Although temperatures can fall below -29 degrees at night, infantry work makes you sweat...This 2RGJ section commander, in snow camouflage clothing and COP vest, wears a privately-purchased *shemagh* – as popular a piece of kit among British soldiers in freezing Norway as in the deserts of the Middle East.
With due respect to 3 Commando Bde, the British AMF(L) components are the only complete units of the British forces doing annual winter and arctic warfare training. The annual exercise "Heartfull", which is independent of the overall AMF(L) training schedule, takes place in northern Norway over six weeks every spring.

Scimitar CVR(T) of 2RGJ guarding Bardufoss airfield, Norway, during "Arctic Express 94". The 7.8-ton Scimitar, with a three-man crew, 30mm Rarden gun, 2x4 smoke grenade launchers and a 7.62mm MG, is capable of speeds up to 80km/h (49mph). The warhorse of the recce platoon, it can also manoeuvre to delay any enemy advance.

(Right, below & opposite) Graffiti on the left side of the turret rear storage bins of the 2RGJ Scimitars during their AMF(L) service, referring to platoon personalities or anecdotes....

(**Above**) The recce platoon of 3 Para, who took over the AMF(L) rotation from 2RGJ, is equipped with Sabre instead of Scimitar. Sabre is basically a Scorpion chassis mounted with the turret of the Fox wheeled armoured car. This also has the L21 Rarden cannon, but backed by an electrically powered L94A1 McDonnell-Douglas 7.62mm "chain gun" in place of the conventional gas-operated GPMG. Further improvements are a new gun catch for better driver vision, new light clusters, a couple of new storage bins, and a new domed hatch for the gunner.

(Above) 2RGJ mortar crew await a fire order during an exercise in Denmark, the first bomb ready, a second close at hand. The mortar platoon of the support company of the British infantry battalion under AMF(L) command has nine L16A1 81mm tubes; each crew can fire up to 15 high explosive, smoke or illumination rounds per minute, out to a maximum range of 5,800 meters.

(Above right) "Bomb gone!" During "Ardent Ground 97" in Turkey the mortar platoon of 2 Para deployed with AMF(L) as 3 Para were on duty in Ulster; note the tropical shirts - summer temperatures in Turkey can easily top 30 C (86 F). Safety drills call for the loader to slide both hands down the outside of the barrel after inserting the bomb; this ensures that he does not accidentally put one over the muzzle. To protect themselves from blast the crew must keep their heads below muzzle level.

(Right) The LAW80 infantry section light anti-tank weapon has an effective range against conventional armoured vehicles of anything from 20m to 500m; it weighs 10kg (22lbs). Note the Union Jack flash untypically worn on this Green Jacket's para smock during exercise "Action Express 93" in Denmark.

(Above) The British infantry battalion's main anti-tank defence is provided by the Milan ATGW system (though this is soon to be replaced by the Trigat MR). Milan can be mounted on a Land Rover, as here by 2RGJ, or on the roof of a BV206 snow-track. The shaped-charge warhead has a flight time of about 12.5 seconds to a target at 2,000m range.

(Right) The Milan crew is normally two; on the march one carries the launcher post (16.4kg - 36lbs), the other two rockets (24.46kg - 54lbs) and the MIRA thermal imaging sight, seen here mounted on a Milan of 3 Para in Norway. British Milans are cooled by gas canisters, visible here at the rear; German Milans use a small generator.

(Above) "Northern options" contingents use the BV206 as a section vehicle and in many other roles; here the rear car serves as a firing platform for the 81mm mortar. Note the normal baseplate of the mortar attached to the rear of the vehicle. In case of need the mortar can be man-packed, with some immediate use ammunition, in three loads.

(Left) During "Strong Resolve 95" in Norway an element of 2RGJ have captured an "enemy" supply convoy; a rifleman covers a comrade while prisoners are searched - note the maps and other papers taken for further examination by the AMF(L) intelligence section. The rifleman wears the chest webbing and day pack which are more popular among British infantry than regulation PLCE 90 kit; the SA80 5.56mm assault rifle is camouflaged with white tape.

(Right) Men of 3 Para leave the LZ after insertion behind enemy lines by German helicopters, to clear key targets such as bridges in preparation for an AMF(L) counterattack. They move fast on snowshoes, despite heavy bergens, sleeping and bivvy bags, insulation matresses, snow shovels and warm layered clothing. They are armed with SA80, LSW, GPMG, LAW80 and Milan.

Luxembourg

Although the smallest NATO nation, Luxembourg contributes a contingent to the AMF(L) force pool. From 1967 until 1985 this was the 1st (LU) Infantry Battalion; since 1985 it has been the reconnaissance company of the 1st Light Infantry Battalion from Diekirch. Although small, this contingent of professional soldiers enjoys a high scale of armament and vehicles and makes a versatile contribution. The unit can be chosen for all AMF(L) options and is completely trained and equipped for arctic warfare. The company is divided into two recce platoons and an anti-tank platoon, each with 37 personnel and HMMWV vehicles.

Since Luxembourg has no military industry much of the army's equipment and vehicles are American-made. Despite this the government chose the Austrian-made Steyr AUG 5.56mm assault rifle to replace their previous FAL rifles and UZI submachine guns. Each HMMWV is equipped with the slightly heavier light machine gun version of the AUG. The six Hummers of the anti-tank platoon are armed with TOW, the others with .50cal machine guns.

An additional mortar platoon has reinforced the company since 1988. This is 46 strong, and consists of three sections each with two L16A2 81mm mortars, and two FOO teams. The platoon moves in eleven HMMWVs, two Mercedes G-Wagons and four MAN trucks.

(Left) Recce trooper, in Canadian snow suit, aiming through the x1.5 optical sight fitted in the carrying handle of his Steyr AUG; with 30 rounds the rifle weighs 4.34kg (9.5lbs).

(Right) The anti-tank platoon's TOWs have a range of between 65m and 3,950m; the launcher takes both the basic 22.5kg (49.6lb) BGM71A and the 28.1kg (62lb) BMG71E. Note Luxembourg cap badge on British-style beret; all the duchy's soldiers are professionals, signing contracts at first for 18 months and thereafter annually.

(Opposite & left) Luxembourg and Dutch vehicles follow advancing Dutch and German infantry during "Adventure Express 97", when the Luxembourg company acted as an anti-armour reserve. Three versions of the four-man HMMWV can be seen - .50cal MG, TOW, and command post. Note NATO camouflage scheme.

Deterrence

As soon as the first fighting units reach the operational area they begin their deterrence operations. As AMF(L) mirrors NATO's doctrine of deterrence, one of the main missions of the advance contingents is to show the flag, both literally and figuratively. During this phase you see the flags of the participating nations on all vehicles and in the holding areas; this is to emphasise to the potential aggressor that he would not be fighting the threatened state alone but all its NATO partners.

While the advance contingents set up the TOC, staging area and LOG-Base, the first combat elements - the so-called "key companies" - move to their operational areas and carry out extensive patrolling. They make an ostensible show of their weapons and equipment to the local population, and the potential aggressor is reminded of the effectiveness of AMF(L) by live firing exercises and weapons effect displays. Humanitarian help, medical support, road-building, sports contests, concerts of military music and parades all contribute to a simultaneous "hearts and minds" programme, to develop good relationships with the local population and to remind them that as citizens of a NATO nation they can count upon the support of all their partner nations.

Exercises and operations provide the only opportunities for extensive cross-training with units of other contingents, and AML(F) makes intensive use of them to hone their co-operation down to the level of the individual soldier - with other AMF(L) contingents, with AMF(A), and with host nation units. Behind the scenes the key companies also prepare for the defensive combat operations which may become necessary, and reconnoitre the surrounding terrain. During this deterrence phase units may also be confronted with anti-NATO demonstrations, sabotage, enemy troops operating under cover, the violation of borders, refugee problems and the shutdown of border crossings.

The actions of AMF(L) during the deterrence phase are controlled by a special set of rules of engagement set up by the NATO High Council and SACEUR. These rules define clearly all levels of escalation which may occur during the deterrence phase. If deterrence fails, they are superseded by the NATO rules of engagement for armed conflicts; if deterrence succeeds, de-escalation begins in co-operation with the host nation.

A measure of deterrence is already provided during peacetime by the five annual AMF(L) exercises - the message they send to potential aggressors is as important as their training aspects. The series features a field training exercise and a command post exercise in different operational zones; a live firing exercise together with AMF(A) to practise co-operation with fire support units; at least one exercise practising the planning and preparation of a deployment; and an exercise to improve the flow of information inside the HQ.

(**Left**) Showing the flag - the panel and flag on this BV206 clearly identify it as belonging to AMF(L) and the German Bundeswehr. The NCO section leader and his machine gunner cover their dismounted comrades who are checking a nearby bridge.

(**Above**) Depending on the escalation level, AMF(L) troops like these Italian Alpini can be used to check civilian traffic behind a threatened border. Their task is to spot enemy infiltrators, smugglers carrying weapons for local guerrilla groups, etc. Their BV206 mounts a TOW.

(**Right**) The particular environment of the deployment area can offer opportunities for cross-training. Here British paratroopers practise ice climbing - an essential skill for troops operating north of the Arctic circle - under the guidance of Royal Netherlands Marine instructors.

Activities in the Deterrence Phase

As an example, the following activities were carried out during the deterrence phase of exercise "Strong Resolve 95":

Live firing of hand weapons

Exchange of infantry sections between different nations, and conduct of joint patrols

Anti-NBC training together with host nation units and the force anti-NBC unit

Challenge Cup competition between AMF(L) units, each nation entering one platoon: running/skiing, shooting, and confidence course

March & Shoot artillery and mortar competition, against the clock

Airlift training with Force Helicopter Unit

Ski and snowshoe training in co-operation with host nation

FAC training

Parachuting, with possibility of acquiring other nations' parachute wings

Weapons and equipment displays to politicians, local dignitaries, in schools and to the population, combined with explanations by officers

Exercise "Arty Barbara": live firing display by Force Artillery and AMF(A), including fast deployment of guns and crews by helicopter

Parade displays

Concerts by military bands of different nations

Common services

Visits to old peoples' homes to inform and deliver humanitarian help

(Opposite top) During the deterrence phase local inhabitants can get a good look at the NATO equipment deployed for their defence. This British 105mm Light Gun - note spiked tyres - has a set of skis which can be mounted under the wheels for towing over deep snow by the BV206.

(Far left) A Norwegian youngster is given a quick lesson on the German 7.62mm MG3 (note AA sight) mounted on a Fuchs wheeled APC. This is basically the excellent World War II-vintage MG42, with a rate of fire of up to 1,200rpm. Bundeswehr infantry use it on a bipod, giving an effective range of 600m; this doubles when it is mounted on a sustained fire tripod or a vehicle.

(Left) 3 Para's hand weapons display during the deterrence phase of "Adventure Express 97". From front to back of the table are a white L96A1 sniper's rifle; a second, camouflaged, and fitted with the Pilkington Kite IWS night sight; and the Light Support Weapon with SUSAT sight. The left-handed Norwegian is trying out the SA80, also fitted here with the Kite IWS.

(Above) Engaging an enemy vehicle during an exercise in Denmark, this Royal Netherlands Marine displays his Corps' dark blue beret with red flash and gold crowned anchor badge. The 84mm Carl Gustav M2 anti-tank weapon was first produced as long ago as 1948, and - despite its teeth-loosening detonation - has proved effective against enemy armour and bunkers ever since. High Explosive Anti-Tank, HE, smoke and illumination rounds are available, weighing between 3.1kg and 3.3kg (6.8lbs - 7.3lbs).

Netherlands

The Netherlands contingent under AMF(L) command is provided by elements of the Royal Netherlands Marine Corps, namely:
2nd Marine Battalion
2nd Mortar Battery
National Support Element

The Royal Netherlands Marine Corps can trace its history back to a decree of December 1665. At first sent into battle against England, since a peace treaty of 1674 the Dutch Marines have often fought side by side with British troops in various campaigns. While the main strength of the Marine Corps forms part of NATO's UK/Netherlands Landing Force, based on Britain's 3 Commando Brigade, other elements provide one of the elite infantry assets of AMF(L) in its northern deployment areas.

The **2nd Marine Bn** consists of three rifle companies (21, 22 and 23 Cos), a support company (24 Co), and a mixed HQ and service company (20 Company). Each 113-strong company consists of three rifle platoons, and an HQ platoon combining the command element, an anti-tank team with a Carl Gustav 84mm ATW, a 60mm mortar team, and medical and signals teams. The rifle platoon consists of three eight-man sections armed with a mixture of C7A1 assault rifles and compatible light machine guns, and one FN MAG 7.62mm machine gun; AT4 light anti-tank weapons are issued at need. In the 124-strong support company an HQ element commands a mortar platoon with six 81mm L16A1 tubes, an anti-tank platoon with 18 Dragon ATGW systems, and a 22-man reconnaissance platoon including four sniper teams equiped with Steyr SSG 69 rifles. The HQ and service company combines all necessary logistical elements.

To guard the command posts each rifle company has a guard section, the battalion CP has a guard platoon, and the HQ and service company two guard platoons; altogether these guard elements have 12 Browning .50cal M2HB machine guns. For fighting at night and in poor visibility 109 passive night vision goggles are held, 13 of them thermal imaging systems, and 62 capable of mounting on infantry weapons.

If the mission requires it other Marine Corps assets can be attached to the battalion: e.g., an anti-aircraft section with 16 men and four Stinger systems; an assault engineer platoon; or the 2nd Boat Troop, with six LCVP (Landing Craft Vehicle/Personnel), with which it is possible to land two marine companies at once.

The **2nd Mortar Bty** is subordinate to Force Artillery AMF(L) and not to the Marine infantry battalion. Its structure is very similar to a British Light Gun battery due to the close co-operation between the Royal Netherlands Marines and the British Royal Marine Commandos. It fields six 120mm tubes in its mortar section and three FOO teams in the tactical HQ section, which also incorporates the battery command posts. The fire direction and FOO teams, as well as the survey team, use laser range-finders, thermal imaging systems and satellite navigation systems. This battery provides most effective fire support to AMF(L) infantry units.

(**Above left**) During "Action Express 93" in Denmark, an NCO of a Marine company HQ platoon readies a hand-held 60mm Thomson-Brandt Commando mortar; weighing only 8kg (17.6lbs), this has a range of 1,050 meters. The close relationship with Britain in UK NLLF is echoed by common use of clothing and equipment; note British- and Dutch-made DPM trousers, and Mk 6 helmets. The national flash is worn on the right shoulder above a drab AMF(L) patch, and the title KORPS MARINIERS on the left. The officer - note naval-style ranking - carries the 9mm UZI, since replaced by the C7A1 rifle.

(**Left**) Marines of the 2nd Mortar Bty, Force Artillery, wear NBC suits as they re-align one of their six 120mm Thomson-Brandt M0 120 RT wheeled tubes. This massive 582kg (1,283lb) weapon has a range of 13km (8 miles) and a normal firing rate of 10 to 12 rounds - HE, smoke, illumination, etc. - each minute. It is usually towed by the Mercedes G-Wagon or BV206.

(**Above right**) The only immediate difference between British troops and these Royal Netherlands Marines skiing through the Norwegian forest is their armament - not, as might appear, US M16s, but a mix of 5.56mm C7A1 assault rifles and light machine guns made by Diemaco in Canada. Both the 4.5kg (9.9lb) rifle and the 6.2kg (13.6lb) LMG version are magazine-fed and fitted with x3.4 Wildcat optical sights, here with protective covers.

(**Right**) Although their individual weapons are now 5.56mm calibre, the Marine section still carries one FN MAG 7.62mm machine gun, virtually identical to those used by Belgian and British troops.

(Above) An anti-tank team from 2nd Bn's support company lie in wait for enemy armour in a Norwegian valley. The AT platoon has 18 of these US-made Dragon systems; at 15.4kg (34lbs) it can be carried by a single soldier. The wire-guided rocket can penetrate even reactive armour at ranges up to 1,000m; it is fitted here with the improved daytime tracker, but a night tracker is also available.

(Left) At need a light air defence detachment of four teams armed with Stinger can be attached to the Royal Netherlands Marines AML(F) contingent; this weapon is widely used by contributing nations. The total weight of the launcher and its 3kg (6.6lb) HE/fragmentation round is 15.7kg (34.6lbs). It has a range of 4,500m up to an altitude of 3,800m (12,500 feet).

On Parade

The parades mounted by AMF(L) in the deployment area make a psychological contribution to the deterrence phase; they "show the flag" in a literal sense. All the AMF(L) nations provide representatives, and there is always a contingent from the host nation. The flag party which leads onto the parade ground shows the NATO and AMF(L) flags and the flags of those AMF(L) nations which are not partaking in the operation.

Usually AMF(L) is put under command of a host nation formation of at least corps size at the parade, and by taking the parade the COMAMF(L) and the host nation commander demonstrate this formally. Official command language during the parade is English, the commanders of the partaking units repeating the orders in their national languages.

(**Right**) Followed by national contingents, the flag party enters the parade ground.

(**Below**) Belgian Para-Commandos give COMAMF(L) and a regional NATO commander "eyes right" and a salute.

(**Below right**) "Present arms!" - a lance-corporal of 2nd Royal Green Jackets faces the icy wind during a parade in Norway; note AMF(L) patch on his windproof smock.

Germany

Since the birth of AMF(L) Germany has provided troops to the force pool; at the time of writing this contingent comprised the following units:

Gebirgsjägerbataillon 233 (Mountain Inf Bn 233)
Fallschirmjägerbataillon 263 (Airborne Inf Bn 263)
2./Batterie, Raketenartilleriebataillon 122 (2 Bty, Rocket Artillery Bn 122)
Luftlandefernmeldekompanie 9 (Airborne Signal Co 9)
Heeresfliegerstaffel 9 (Army Air Sqn 9)
3./Kompanie ABC-Abwehrbataillon 7 (3 Co, Anti-NBC Bn 7)
Luftlandesanitätskompanie 260 (Airborne Medical Co 260)
National Support Element

Mountain Inf Bn 233 took over the AMF(L) mission from Airborne Inf Bn 252, which was disbanded shortly afterwards. The 990-strong battalion has four equally structured 148-strong rifle companies, backed by a support company and an HQ and service company. The rifle company consists of four platoons each with three Fuchs APCs, and a command section with an additional Fuchs. For deployments to northern Norway, for which its training fits it well, the battalion can also make use of BV206 over-snow vehicles. The companies of the battalion have a total of 16 Milan ATGW systems, and the Panzerfaust 3 ATW is also in use.

The battalion's heavy support company combines a mortar platoon with six 120mm tubes; an anti-tank platoon with six Wiesel weapons carriers equipped with TOW; a cannon platoon with six Wiesels equipped with 20mm cannon; and an HQ and service platoon. Apart from all elements required for command and services, the HQ and service company also contains the high mountain platoon. This is drawn from specially trained mountain and Arctic warfare instructors, and is responsible for reconnaissance and pathfinding in mountainous terrain.

If **Airborne Inf Bn 263** deploys under the "southern option", one of the airborne infantry companies is detached and a Wiesel company from Fallschirmpanzerabwehrbataillon 262 (Airborne Anti-Tank Bn 262) is substituted, serving alongside three equally structured rifle companies and the HQ and service company.

Each rifle company has a company HQ and three rifle platoons, each with three sections and an HQ element. Two of the platoon's sections, carried in Unimog cross-country vehicles or BV206 snow-tracks, number ten men armed with nine G3 7.62mm assault rifles, an MG3 machine gun, a 40mm grenade launcher and a Panzerfaust 3 ATW. (In the near future the 5.56mm G36 will replace the G3 rifle.) The sections use the SEM 52 radio set, and the platoon HQ the SEM 70. The third rifle section uses a Mercedes G-Wagon carrying a Milan ATGW and a three-man crew, and a Unimog with a seven-man crew; personal weapons are the same as in the other sections. Subordinate to the company HQ section are two snipers with the accurized sniper version of the G3; when the G3 is taken out of service the Accuracy L96A1 will replace this. The company HQ section is also equipped with an MG3 and the SEM 70 radio set.

The battalion is reinforced by an airborne engineer platoon

(Opposite top) Men of Airborne Mortar Co 260 set up in a new position. Each mortar section comprises five men with three Mercedes G-Wagons (termed the "Wolf" in army service). One carries the Soltan 120mm light mortar with five rounds, the other two 49 HE, smoke and illumination rounds; in 1998 a new armour-piercing/fragmentation round will be issued. Note new camouflage fatigues, ballistic helmets and body armour.

(Above) Alternatively the mortar platoon can be airlifted by FHU. In the lift net a pallet forms the load base (ammo is stacked on this in the firing position). The baseplate is stowed on the pallet, followed by the bipod, barrel, storage box for small items, boxed R16A1 periscope sight, the section's light ATW and five rucksacks, camo net, digging tools, and ten rounds; total weight is 380kg (838lbs).

(Above right) One mortar is already being manhandled into "line of sight" while the second is assembled, and the third is just about to be lowered into position by its blue marker flag.

(Right) Night firing; note two crewmen pressing down on the bipod to stop it jumping, and white-coded illumination rounds in background. With the M48 round the maximum range is 6,250 meters.

31

from Luftlandepionierkompanie 260 (who also reinforce the mountain infantry battalion in case of the "northern option"). Also attached to the airborne infantry battalion is a platoon from Luftlandemörserkompanie 260 with 51 soldiers and four 120mm mortars in four mortar teams, an HQ element, two observer teams, a fire direction centre and a medical section, as well as parts of the company HQ and service platoon.

Since spring 1997 Germany also provides the **anti-NBC component** of AMF(L) with a mixed platoon from 3. Kompanie ABC-Abwehrbataillon 7. This enables AMF(L) to continue its mission even under NBC conditions. The 48-strong platoon is capable of monitoring combat gas and nuclear fallout from its Fuchs armoured NBC recce vehicles, and in some circumstances can neutralise what it detects, e.g. by establishing and operating a main decontamination station for personnel and material. Other platoon missions may include fire-fighting and the transport of water.

Just as the Italian contingent provides the **medical element** for AMF(L) southern options, so Germany's Luftlandesanitätskompanie 260 now fills this role for the northern options (taking over the mission from 2./ Kompanie Sanitätslehrbataillon 851 - 2 Co, Medical Training Battalion 851). Together with a field hospital with 80 places the company can establish a clearing station with 20 places, and has an ambulance platoon with ten vehicles. Apart from providing medical care in peacetime and war for all AMF(L) national contingents, the company is also in charge of food control, dental treatment, and the evacuation of casualties in co-operation with IALCE.

(Above) While the paratroopers have only 2-ton Unimog trucks and BV206s, Mountain Inf Bn 233 has the amphibious six-wheel Fuchs APC - combat weight 18,300kg (18 tons), 12 man capacity, top road speed 105km/h (65mph).

(Opposite top) Fuchs mounts MG3s front and rear and a Milan centrally. Foreground, TOW-armed Wiesel of 233 Bn's support company, with three-man crew and internal/external stowage for seven missiles; combat weight 2.8 tons; range 300km (186 miles); top speed 75km/h (46mph).

The German national support element is provided by Luftlandeversorgungskompanie 260 (Airborne Supply Co 260). In close co-operation with the British CSS Bn they handle the German troops' needs for fast resupplies of fuel, provisions, spares, ammunition, etc.

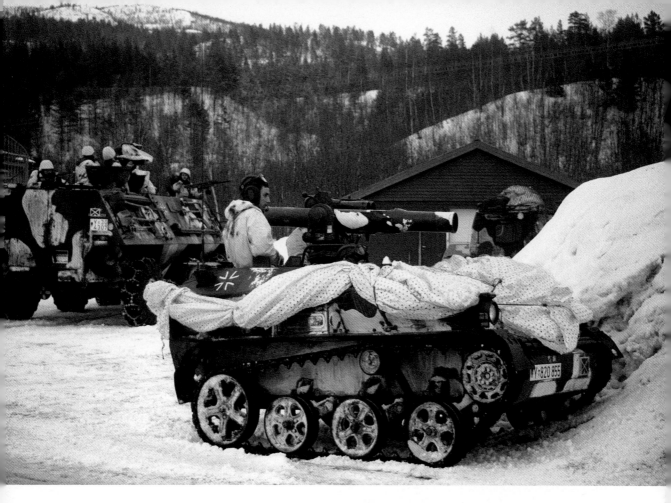

(Below) Section of German paratroopers moving up to a ridge position, followed by an artillery observer's Wolf. They wear peaked camouflage field caps badged with the national cockade, green-spotted snow camo suits and Canadian boots, and carry G3A3 rifles, MG3, Panzerfaust 3, and a grenade launcher.

(Below right) Mountain infantryman of 233 Bn advances on skis to a new fire position. Note his new webbing equipment in camouflage finish, additionally camouflaged with white tape - like his G3 assault rifle. Although mostly conscripts fulfilling their ten months' military service like most other German soldiers, mountain infantry are mainly drawn from Bavaria and other mountainous southern regions and many learn skiing and climbing skills from childhood. During their service they are thoroughly trained in winter conditions and mountain terrain.

(Above) Airborne Wiesel with 20mm Rheinmetall MK20 RH 202 cannon; this two-man version carries 160 rounds of various types, easily changed by use of a dual feed system. Wiesels mounting the 120mm mortar and the Stinger are awaited. Note cobra badge painted on turret.

(Left) FOO team with Wild TAS 10 target acquisition system incorporating laser range-finder, electronic goniometer and azimuth gyroscope; this fulfills all observation, orientation, measurement, data processing and transfer functions. This old steel helmet has now been replaced by the ballistic "Fritz".

(Below left) The 110mm Panzerfaust 3 weighs 12.9kg (28lbs); combat range is 300-500m, and it can even be fired from inside a room - backblast prevents this with many such light AT weapons.

From 1 July 1998 the AMF(L) mission will pass from Luftlandebrigade 26 to Jägerbrigade 37, and the mission for the southern option will be taken over by **Fallschirmjägerbataillon 373**; the brigade units of the airborne brigade will hand over their missions to the equivalent units of the light infantry brigade. As **Gebirgsjägerbataillon 571** (Mountain Inf Bn 571) is part of 37 Light Infantry Brigade, it is likely that it will take over the northern option mission from Mountain Inf Bn 233.

Fallschirmjagerbataillon 373 is differently structured from other German airborne infantry battalions. It consists of an HQ and service company, three equally structured rifle companies, and a heavy company. The heavy company combines two mortar platoons with five 120mm tubes each; two anti-tank platoons with four TOW Wiesels each; and two cannon platoons each with four 20mm cannon Wiesels.

Turkey

Since 1996 Turkey, in whose territory many of the contingency areas of AMF(L) are located, puts under AMF(L) command one artillery battery and one engineer company from the 41st Infantry Brigade, and a national support element. The 118-strong artillery battery is equipped with six M101 105mm towed howitzers. The 143-man engineer company fields nine engineer vehicles for different earth-moving tasks, as well as mining and mine clearance equipment. Both the engineers and the gunners are stationed at Vize in north-western Turkey; most of the soldiers are conscripts.

(Below) The battery's M101 howitzers and their eight-man crews are towed and transported by Mercedes Benz L1300 Unimog trucks. The 2.26-ton guns, covered here against dust, have a maximum range of 11,270m and can fire at a rate of up to ten rounds per minute.

(Right) "Ardent Ground 97", Turkey: this gunner, displaying the AMF(L) patch on a parka in distinctive Turkish camouflage, has a differing US-style pattern helmet cover. He carries a licence-made G3 rifle; a few moments ago four "enemy" were caught infiltrating his battery position.

Denmark

At the moment Denmark provides one of the smallest contingents under AMF(L) command: one platoon from the reconnaissance company of the Bornholm Combat Group, and a national support element. The platoon has two officers and 40 NCOs and enlisted men; nine MOWAG Eagle reconnaissance vehicles, introduced by the Danish army in 1996, and a Mercedes G-Wagon command vehicle. The platoon can be divided into two independently operating recce groups. Although only raised in 1986, this unit's soldiers have been deployed to Bosnia with IFOR and SFOR; and in 1994 they prepared Lithuanian soldiers for their mission as part of IFOR's Nordic-Polish Brigade. (See also Europa-Militaria 22: *IFOR - Allied Forces in Bosnia*)

(Right) Danish radio operator listening to new orders; note the distinctive national camouflage pattern. Not shown here is the 5.56mm Diemaco C7A1 rifle, used by the Danes as well as the Canadians and Dutch.

(Below) MOWAG Eagle of the AMF(L) unit, here serving with IFOR in Bosnia. Based on the HMMWV, the 4,800kg (10,580lb) 4x4 Eagle is armoured, has an NBC overpressure system, and mounts an observation turret; it carries a crew of four. (Photo courtesy Yves Debay)

Force Artillery AMF(L)

Force Artillery AMF(L) is the brigade's multinational artillery battalion, led by an HQ battery from Great Britain. Up to seven artillery batteries from Canada, Germany, Greece, Italy, Spain, Turkey, Great Britain and the USA may be subordinated to HQ Force Artillery, plus the Dutch 120mm mortar battery; normally, however, the HQ commands four batteries.

HQ Force Arty is in charge of co-ordinating the fire of the subordinate batteries; this co-ordination task may additionally embrace supporting fire from naval vessels and close air support, as well as host nation units and NATO units which are not directly subordinate to HQ Force Artillery. HQ Force Arty also advises COMAMF(L) on questions of artillery operations; reconnoitres and surveys fire positions; monitors weather conditions; and operates the Fire Direction Centre (FDC), which also co-ordinates fire missions with FASC. The FDC attaches FOO teams to the combat battalions, to direct supporting fire for the infantry in the front line.

The following descriptions cover the British and German batteries; other batteries are described elsewhere under their respective nations.

The most powerful and long-ranged unit of the Force

110mm rockets thunder into the sky above the Turkish/Iraqi borderlands from a Bundeswehr MAN 7-ton LARS launcher truck; this has two stacks each of 18 tubes, and can release all 36 in 18 seconds, out to ranges of 8,000 to 14,000 meters.

Artillery is **2./Batterie, Raketenartilleriebataillon 122** of the German Bundeswehr, stationed at Walldüren. (The rocket battery took over the AMF(L) mission from the since-disbanded Luftlandeartilleriebatterie 9 - Airborne Arty Bty 9 - which was equipped with six 105mm pack howitzers and could provide three FOO teams.) The battery has two rocket launcher platoons each with four 110mm LARS launchers and two FERA fire direction radars; a medical troop; and an ammunition troop with four cross-country 10-ton lorries. The battery HQ combines two fire direction teams with ARES and two reconnaissance teams; a maintenance and repair platoon completes the structure of the battery.

LARS is used against area targets, one of its main tasks being the rapid spreading of area denial munitions. During battle the battery supports the infantry units by firing HE/fragmentation rockets, multiple mines, and smoke to hinder enemy movement, blind their forces, and destroy their positions and forces in previously specified areas, such as gaps in a front line and on its flanks.

The battery's fire position area covers four square kilometers, containing three fire positions, the battery command post, and a staging area with a loading position; its preparation takes one to two hours. The time from receiving a fire mission to commiting is about 40 minutes; during this time up to 36 rockets per

launcher are loaded by hand, the battery moves into the fire position, and the launchers are aimed.

Great Britain's **5 (Gibraltar) Field Battery**, stationed at Larkhill, has six 105mm Light Guns and can provide four FOO teams equipped with PRC352 and PRC320 radios as well as OTIS (Observer Thermal Imaging System), LRF (Laser Range Finder) and MSTAR (Manportable Surveillance Target Acquisition Radar). The six-man gun crews and their equipment are transported in BV206s, or the newly introduced Pinzgauer cross-country vehicle with a payload of 1.4 tonnes. The battery fields two platoons with three guns each, the battery command post with fire direction crews, and the supply element with the ammunition section.

Like most 105mm batteries within AMF(L), 5 (Gibraltar) Field Battery is completely airportable. It can be transported by helicopter to conduct fire missions, being ready to engage shortly after guns, personnel, ammunition and the battery command post have been dropped. The British battery is not the only one to need less than a minute from receiving a fire mission to firing the first rounds; the multinational Force Artillery gives AMF(L) a powerful punch, easy to move and quick to deliver.

(**Opposite top**) Soldiers of 2nd Bty, Rocket Arty Bn 122 load fragmentation rockets. The battery's eight 10-ton ammo trucks carry 144 rockets each; with the eight loaded launchers this gives a total of 1,440, enough for five complete series - 720 mine-distribution rounds, 576 fragmentation, and 144 smoke. Two FERA fire direction radars are carried on the same model MAN 7 trucks. The radar follows the trajectory of four ranging rounds, and calculates any difference between planned and actual trajectory; the correction forms the basis for the final fire order. The launcher trucks have a loaded weight of 15,900kg (15.6 tons), top road speed of 90km/h (56mph), and a road range of 550km (340 miles).

(**Above**) Observers from different contingents often guide the fire of Force Arty guns and mortars of four or more nations as they give a single target that wasteland experience....Here a Spanish FOO (left, with Steiner binoculars) and a Belgian (right, with laser range-finder) control British, German and Italian guns in Turkey.

(**Opposite below**) Royal Artillery personnel from HQ Force Arty survey gun positions in Norway, 1995, with Leica Wild SKK 3 azimuth gyroscope.

(**Right**) "Fire for effect!" - an empty is ejected from an L118A1 105mm Light Gun of 5 (Gibraltar) Bty RA. This British weapon weighs 1.86 tons and has a range of up to 17,300 meters. HE, smoke and illumination rounds consist of the projectile, case, and one of seven differently-ranged charges. The gun can be fired from a traverse plate which is stowed on the trail for transport, when the barrel is reversed to point toward the tow vehicle.

Belgium

Apart from the national support element the Belgian contingent comprises an infantry battalion selected, depending upon availability, from the following units of the Brigade Para-Commando:

    1ste Bataljon Parachutisten
    2e Bataillon Commando
    3de Bataljon Parachutisten

Although the terms Parachutist and Commando are retained for traditional reasons, all three battalions are in fact equally structured para-commando units. Each battalion has an HQ, service and support company and three rifle companies. The support element comprises a mortar platoon fielding either six NR 475A1 PR8 81mm or six M30 107mm tubes, depending on the nature of the mission; an anti-tank platoon with Milan ATGWs mounted on VW Iltis vehicles; and a reconnaissance platoon equipped with VW Iltis armed with .50cal machine guns.

Each of the three rifle companies has a command section numbering 15 men and including a 60mm mortar. The company's two rifle platoons each have a command element and three ten-man sections. Two of these sections are armed with a 7.62mm belt-fed FN MAG, a 5.56mm Minimi LMG with alternative belt or magazine feed, a 7.62mm L96A1 sniper rifle, and seven 5.56mm FNC assault rifles; the third has two additional Milan posts. M62 rifle grenades can be used with the FNC, and

(**Above**) Para-Commandos crew an FN MAG to cover their section's advance; the tripod mount extends the effective range from 800 to 1,800 metres.

(**Right**) Patrolling during the deterrence phase of a deployment on the coast of Zeeland, this Para-Commando wears a Goretex jacket in US camouflage pattern over his Belgian camo suit. The 5.56mm FNC assault rifle has

replaced the FN FAL in Belgian service; it has a 30-round magazine, an "iron" sight and a folding butt. The 1st and 3rd Bns of the Bde Para-Cdo wear paratrooper red berets, the 2nd Bn commando green, for reasons of historical tradition. All wear a winged dagger cap badge based on that of the British SAS - enlisted men in brass, NCOs in silver and officers in gilt.

for light anti-tank purposes the 66mm M72 LAW is issued.

In the past Belgium also used to provide the reconnaissance element for AMF(L) in the form of an armoured recce company from 1ste Regiment Jagers te Paard, fielding eight CVR(T) Scorpion, eight Scimitar and four Spartan. An anti-aircraft element with 12 Mistral systems and early warning radar also used to be under AMF(L) command, but no longer. However, in recent years the artillery battery of the Bde Para-Commando, with eight M101A1 105mm howitzers, Unimog 416 cross-country vehicles and two FOO teams, has frequently taken part in AMF(L) exercises.

(**Above**) Used by the reconnaissance and anti-tank platoons of the Belgian Para-Cdo battalions as a mobile platform for the FN MAG machine gun, as here, or the Milan ATGW, the 4x4 Volkswagen Iltis is manufactured under licence by Bombardier; top speed is 130kp/h (80mph).

(**Left**) Like most NATO armies the Belgians use the Milan ATGW, first combat-proven in the "bunker busting" role by British troops in the 1982 Falklands War. It is seen here fitted with the MIRA thermal imaging sight for night and low-visibility work.

The Belgian Para-Commandos are all professional soldiers, highly trained for insertion and combat in various environments; their personal equipment often shows a degree of individual choice.

(Right) Deterrence patrol from an advance "key company" of the green-beret 2nd Cdo Bn passing through a Turkish village, mounted in a 1.5 ton Unimog truck and armed with FNC rifles and FN MAG machine gun.

(Below) Para-Commandos photographed during cross-training, disembarking from a Royal Netherlands Marines Boat Troop LCVP. The landing craft can carry 35 fully equipped soldiers or a small vehicle with trailer; it has a three-man crew.

Norway

Norway forms the northern flank of NATO and is therefore one of AMF(L)'s most important deployment areas. Since exercise "Strong Resolve 95", which first saw a Norwegian battalion under AMF(L) command, the Telemark Battalion has become part of the force pool. The mission of this mechanized infantry battalion embraces both defence of NATO territory in co-operation with AMF(L) and other forces; and providing units for UN peace-keeping missions, to which the Telemark Bn contributes Norway's contingent.

The battalion is 923 strong, most of them conscripts who volunteer to do their national service in the battalion and to remain on stand-by for an extra 12 months after completing their statutory year. The battalion fields three equally structured rifle companies each of 131 personnel, which are divided into two rifle platoons, an anti-tank platoon and a command section. Two of the three companies are equipped with BV206 Hägglund tracked vehicles, the third with SISU wheeled APCs; there are four vehicles in each platoon and an additional two for the command section. The four rifle sections of a platoon number eight personnel each, armed with an MG3 and seven AG3s (a Norwegian licenced copy of the German G3), one of them fitted with a 40mm grenade launcher. The infantry also use Glock 17 pistols and MP5 sub-machine guns.

The battalion has a 166-strong HQ and service company which includes a signals and a medical platoon; and a support company. This fields a mortar platoon with eight 81mm Royal Ordnance L16A1 tubes transported on BV206s; an anti-tank platoon with four TOW ATGW; an engineer platoon; a FAC team; and a reconnaissance platoon with eight Ranger teams each of four soldiers, each team with two Honda skidoos.

Although the Telemark Bn was only formed in August 1994 it saw its first active service in December 1995, when elements were deployed with the Nordic-Polish Brigade of IFOR. At the time of writing a company of the battalion guards the HQ of LANDCENT in Sarajevo.

(Below) The 16-ton SISU XA185 six-wheeled APC used by one company of the Telemark Bn; in Norwegian service this amphibious carrier has additional armour, and a turret (detail inset) mounting a .50cal MG and eight smoke grenade dischargers. It accomodates two crew and ten riflemen.

(Right) The emerald green beret is the distinction of the Telemark Bn; the title refers to the region where it is stationed. The brass national cap badge bears the cypher of King Haakon V.

(Left) During exercise "Adventure Express 97" elements of the battalion conducted field trials of some 42 items of new Norwegian army combat equipment. These included a new ballistic helmet, new personal load-carrying equipment and body armour, a three-layer glove system, two different sizes of rucksack and a sleeping bag.

45

(Left) The four-man Ranger teams of the Telemark Bn recce platoon each use two Honda Lynx snow scooters; with towed sleighs they can carry all necessary supplies for several days behind enemy lines, and at remarkable speed over rough terrain. The Rangers are tasked with direct action against such targets as bridges and communications centres, as well as with deep reconnaissance.

(Right) The Norwegian army introduced the French Eryx short range anti-tank weapon at section level in 1996, also developing a special tripod. With a weight of 12kg (26lbs) the Eryx has a maximum range of 600m, and can penetrate armour up to 900mm thick; it can also be fired from inside buildings.

Joint Force Helicopter Unit

The Joint Force Helicopter Unit currently consists of four Pumas of 33 Sqn RAF stationed at RAF Odiham in Hampshire, and 12 Bell UH-1Ds of the Leichte Heeresfliegertransportstaffel 9 (AMF(L)) from Niederstetten in Germany. (The latter, an independent unit since 1993, will be disbanded during 1998 and its mission will pass to another Bundeswehr aviation unit.) In the operational area their command posts combine to form HQ JFHU, under tactical command of COMAMF(L). Apart from the service element of the German squadron, which contains all necessary supply, maintenance and medical units, JFHU is supported by a British Tactical Supply Wing and 244 Signal Squadron.

A third helicopter component has been a trio of UH-1Hs provided by 5/158 Aviation Rgt of 12 (US) Aviation Bde, as airmobile command posts for COMAMF(L). The unit is currently re-equipping with Black Hawk, its AMF(L) mission passing to 6th Aviation Regt (SETAF). The US helicopters are directly subordinate to COMAMF(L) and not to HQ JFHU.

The most important in the range of missions conducted by

(**Above**) The helicopters cannot always touch down to insert troops; if this is impossible for some reason they hover, either a couple of meters off the ground so that the infantry, FOOs or gun crews can jump out; or - as for these Italian Alpini - higher, so that they can abseil down. JFHU can also drop paratroopers, or recover personnel by winching them up.

JFHU is the deployment and air transport of artillery batteries, signals, medics and infantry units; but the job also includes MEDEVAC missions, resupply, reconnaissance, march supervision and SAR missions. In mountainous and forested terrain the helicopters can also be used as advanced observers, co-operating with the FOOs of the Force Artillery.

Co-operation between JFHU and the multinational units requesting helicopter support requires extraordinary capabilities of the pilots, maintenance crews and ground personnel, to ensure the operability of the helicopters, independent of surrounding infrastructure, at anything from -30 degrees in northern Norway to +45 degrees in eastern Turkey.

For AMF(L) deployments SOPs have been established for units requesting transport space from the TOC. This is done in the form of a so-called HelQuest. The Force Air Support Centre (FASC) of 1st UK Group RAF from Odiham - which co-ordinates all air missions by helicopters as well as jets - forwards the approved requests to the HQ JFHU, which allocates the transport space in the form of the correct number of Hueys or Pumas to transport the given load. This allocation, the so-called HelTask, contains number and type of helicopters, pick-up point and landing site, mission, radio frequencies, units to be transported, tactical situation and timings for the operation.

(**Left**) Crewman in one of the three UH-1Hs provided by the US Army's 6th Aviation Regt for COMAMF(L)'s use as command platforms, VIP transport, etc.; note AMF(L) metal badge and helmet sticker, national and unit patches. He wears a crew survival vest containing emergency rations, first aid kit, knife, survival blanket, flares, and so on.

(**Right**) Puma of No 33 Sqn RAF - note stag's head badge - waiting for the last of a stick of infantrymen to stow their rucksacks before taking off. The twin-engined Puma has a crew of four and takes 16 fully equipped soldiers, or six stretcher cases and six sitting casualties; maximum payload of 3.8 tons includes an underslung load capacity of 3.2 tons, so a 1.8-ton 105mm gun is no problem.

(**Left**) To load this despatch rider's Herkules K125 motorcycle inside, the seats have been removed from this Heeresflieger Bell UH-1D. Normally the Huey can lift eight fully equipped infantrymen, or six stretcher casualties. The single-engined UH-1D officially has a maximum take-off weight of 4,310kg (9,500lbs) but, taking wind conditions into account, the Bundeswehr pilots often push this to the limit.

"Ardent Ground 97", Turkey: a UH-1D prepares to lift a Spanish Model 56 pack howitzer 10km to a new position - rapid airlifting of artillery batteries is an important tactic in AMF(L) operations. Note the on-board mechanic hanging out the door to check the rigging team below; incorrect rigging of underslung loads leading to instability or rotation can cause serious problems, even a crash. At 1,290kg (2,843lbs) the complete gun is too heavy for the Huey, so the gunshield has been removed; the howitzer can be broken down into 11 sub-assemblies, none weighing more than 122kg (270lbs).

If there are several loads to pick up they are usually lined up 30-50m apart. The pilot approaches into the wind; a marshaller directs him to the furthest load; he touches down briefly to discharge static electricity build-up, then hovers for the pick-up. One rigger can attach the prepared load to the hook; a second sometimes passes hand signals to the crew.

(**Above**) The Tactical Supply Wing can establish a Forward Operation Base or Forward Arming & Refuelling Point in addition to the Main Operation Base, by flying personnel, bulk fuel containers and pumps to some suitable field location; after the operation they can be extracted by air. (Sometimes a FARP can also include tanker vehicles.) The FARP shortens rotation time and frees helicopters as soon as possible for their next mission.

(**Inset**) Badge of Bundeswehr Heeresfliegerstaffel 9.

(**Below**) Some national contingents have their own helicopter assets, like this Bell 206 Jet Ranger attached to the Italian 3rd Alpini.

Background, the USMC maritime command platform USS *Wasp*; for "Strong Resolve 95" II Marine Expeditionary Unit served with the British and Dutch Marines of UK NLLF under AMF(L), which was enlarged to form a divisional HQ.

Portugal

Since 1 January 1997 Portugal provides the long range reconnaissance element for AMF(L). Possible missions for this Special Forces unit (which entered service in 1996) range from reconnaissance behind enemy lines to active operations against e.g. power lines, bridges, military HQs, supply depots, anti-aircraft radars and rocket launchers. Others might include freeing prisoners of war, or engaging enemy snipers. Operation scenarios include infiltration and extraction of teams by sea, air or land. These LRRP teams are trained and equipped to operate self-sufficiently for up to ten days behind enemy lines.

The unit numbers three officers, 30 NCOs and 15 enlisted men. The heart of the unit is a special operations platoon with four operations teams of five soldiers each and a six-man command team. The command team is supported by radio, medical and transport teams; there are two all-terrain vehicles, one heavy and five medium trucks and an ambulance. The soldiers are armed with 7.62mm G3 assault rifles, 9mm UZI sub-machine guns and 7.62mm L96A1 Accuracy sniper rifles; their arsenal also includes 9mm Walther P38s, Israeli Galil assault rifles, silenced MP5s, shotguns and light anti-tank weapons. The broad variety of possible missions, in any terrain from desert to mountain and Arctic, requires a multitude of special equipment, e.g. climbing and diving gear, GPS navigation and satellite communication systems.

During AMF(L) missions the Portuguese Special Forces attach a liaison troop to the command post of AMF(L), to forward important reconnaissance reports as quickly as possible to COMAMF(L) and to ensure that the unit operates according to command requirements.

(Above) The new Portuguese Special Forces unit wears a green beret with a badge combining the Infantry buglehorn and the Commando wreath and dagger.

(Below) The LRRPs used their first deployment to Norway to learn skiing, and to perfect cold weather orientation - challenging for Portuguese soldiers unused to such extremes.

Spain

Although their deployment is subject to special regulations, Spain provides the following units for service with AMF(L):
3 Bandera "Ortiz de Zarate", BRIPAC
BRC II
1 Battery, 1 Mountain Artillery Group
National Support Element

The 3rd Bandera, "Ortiz de Zarate" is one of the Spanish army's three airborne infantry battalions, and is stationed - like the artillery battery – at Alcala de Henares. The 661-man battalion has three rifle companies, an HQ and service company and a support company. The HQ and service company includes logistical and medical components. The support company includes a reconnaissance platoon and a LRRP element, an anti-tank platoon with TOW, an anti-aircraft platoon with Mistral, and a mortar platoon with six 81mm tubes.

The three rifle companies each comprise an HQ platoon, three rifle platoons, and a support platoon with two 81mm mortars, four Milan ATGW posts, and three MG3 machine guns. The soldiers of the three rifle platoons are armed with 5.56mm CETME assault rifles, 5.56mm CETME-L light machine guns, and 90mm C90 LAWs. At the time of writing the battalion was about to hand over its AMF(L) mission to a mountain infantry battalion (Batallon de Casadores de Alta Montana).

Also new to the force pool of AMF(L) is BRC II, an armoured cavalry reconnaissance unit stationed at Zaragoza, which fields 17 CVR(T) Scorpions with 76mm cannon. The last Spanish combat element is a battery of the 1st Mountain Artillery Group with six Otobreda 105mm pack howitzers.

(Opposite top left) These two Portuguese LRRPs, wearing snow clothing provided by the Norwegian army, deliberately moved from their real hide position so as to be visible for the camera.

(Opposite top right) They pose to display the Austrian sleeping bag, snow clothing and body heating system.

(Left) Portuguese Special Forces equipment is acquired from several nations. On operations they carry Berghaus rucksacks, one-man tents, Goretex bivvy bags, camouflage nets, thermal and waterproof clothing, night vision goggles, snowshoes, shovels, GPS sets, and much more. The Goretex waterproof combat clothing is finished in British DPM.

(Above right) The blue vest marks this impressive Spanish senior NCO as the main marshaller on a helicopter LZ, responsible for guiding the choppers by hand signals to the next loading or landing point. His helmet cover, jacket and webbing are finished in a Spanish camouflage pattern similar to the US woodland scheme.

(Right) Spanish mountain gunners set the fuses of 105mm rounds for a direct fire mission; note Spanish army webbing, 5.56mm CETME assault rifle, and insignia of nationality, rank and branch. Their Model 56 pack howitzers take the same range of HE, HEAT, smoke and illumination rounds as the US M101.

(Left) Spanish mountain gunners prepare their position. In this configuration, with the wheels "overslung", the Otobreda Model 56 howitzer has an elevation of +65 to -5 degrees and a traverse of 18 degrees. Range is approximately 10.5km (6.5 miles).

(Right) In the pack configuration with wheels "underslung", as if delivering direct fire on enemy bunkers or armour, elevation decreases to between +25 and -5 degrees but traverse extends to 28 degrees; its HEAT round can penetrate 100mm of armour. This gun is at full recoil; note that while No.1 fires the gun the rest of the crew take cover.

Italy

Italian AMF(L) participation is provided by the "Cuneense Contingent". The name recalls a World War II Alpini Division which distinguished itself on the Eastern Front; but the contingent is formed from parts of the "Taurinese" Bde of the 4th Alpini Corps, comprising the following units:

3rd Alpini Regiment
40 Bty, 1st Mountain Artillery Regt
101st Field Hospital
National Support Element

The 3rd Alpini, from Pinerolo, has belonged to the force pool since 1963; previously known as the "Susa" Alpini Bn, it became a regiment with the restructuring of the Italian forces. The HQ and service company of the former battalion today commands the whole regiment, the battalion no longer having an HQ component of its own. Subordinate to the company are HQ, maintenance, supply, signals, and transport platoons; a reconnaissance platoon with six AutoBlindo Iveco or BV206 vehicles mounting machine guns; and an engineer platoon with two Caterpillar earth-movers.

The **"Susa" Bn** consists of three equally structured rifle companies and a support company. Each rifle company has an HQ and service platoon, three rifle platoons, and an anti-tank platoon with six Milan ATGW posts. The 30-man rifle platoon has three sections, each carrying an MG42/59, a Panzerfaust 3 ATW, a 5.56mm Minimi LMG, and one sniper version of the Beretta SC70/90 rifle, the rest of the section being armed with the conventional model. The section moves in BV206 or Iveco VM90 vehicles. The support company has three heavy mortar platoons each with four 120mm tubes; and an anti-tank platoon with 12 TOW wire-guided ATGWs - six carried on BV206s, six on Fiat AR75s.

The **101a Reparto di Sanita** is structured in two sub-units: a 30-bed clearing station, and a field surgical hospital with 70 beds. Two ambulance points can also be established in the front line, to take over casualties from unit-level medical teams or to support them with personnel and material. The Italian contingent has an integrated helicopter squadron, with two Bell 205 Medevac choppers which are subordinate to the field hospital, and two Bell 206 Jet Ranger reconnaissance machines.

Italy also contributes to the Force Artillery **40 Batteria**, an element of **1a "Aosta" Artiglieria da Montagna**, from Fossano. This fields six Otobreda 105mm pack howitzers, divided between two gun platoons each with their own command post for independent operations; battery HQ also commands three FOO teams.

Due to its mountain training the 3rd Alpini is earmarked for AMF(L)'s northern options; the field hospital, for southern options only; and the artillery can be deployed anywhere.

(Above) On parade Alpini wear the famous mountain hat with a black feather, the blue boss colour here identifying the 3rd Regt; the badge is gold for officers, black for enlisted ranks.

(Below) Sleeve patches worn by 40th Bty, drawn from 1st "Aosta" Mtn Arty Regt.; and by **(bottom)** 3rd Alpini Regt. Note Goretex camouflage jacket in US pattern.

(Left) 40th Bty gunners adjust elevation and bearing of their Model 1956 105mm pack howitzer; this can be fired at a rate of four rounds per minute for 30 minutes, or three per minute for an hour.

(Right) Men of a 3rd Alpini section advance; note German-style snow camouflage suit, with national sleeve flash and sergeant's rank on chest. These soldiers carry 5.56mm Beretta SC70/90 rifles, the 7.62mm MG42/59 (virtually identical to the German MG3), and the Milan ATGW.

Canada

Although Canada has provided troops for all northern options of the AMF(L) since 1964, today units are only earmarked for deployments to northern Norway, as follows:

1st Battalion, The Royal Canadian Regiment
F Battery, 2nd Regt, Royal Canadian Horse Artillery
National Support Element

The **1st Bn, Royal Canadian Regt** took over the AMF(L) mission from 1st Bn, Princess Patricia's Canadian Light Infantry; with F Bty 2RCHA, it is stationed at Petawawa, and comprises four rifle companies, a support company and an HQ and service company. Each rifle company has three rifle platoons, each carried in four BV206s - one for each section, and one for the command element. Rifle platoons carry C7A1 rifles, Minimi LMGs, an 84mm Carl-Gustav ATW and a 60mm mortar. The support company combines an anti-tank platoon with four M113A1 TUA (TOW Under Armour) vehicles, a signals platoon, a mortar platoon with six 81mm tubes, a reconnaissance platoon and an assault pioneer platoon.

For the AMF(L) role an MP section is attached to the battalion HQ. Other detachments put under command of the Canadian infantry battalion can include three Kiowa helicopters of 427 Tactical Helicopter Sqn, a detachment from the 2nd Combat Engineer Regt, and a medical liaison team from 2nd Field Ambulance.

F Battery, 2RCHA is 109 men strong. It consists of an HQ platoon with the logistic element; two artillery platoons each with three 105mm Giat LG1 Mark II Light Guns; and two

artillery observer teams.

To deploy to Europe the Canadian contingent has to travel over 5,000km (3,100 miles). Due to the frequent commitment of Canadian troops to UN missions - e.g. in Bosnia, Cyprus, and Cambodia - as well as to IFOR and SFOR, in recent years only the HQ elements, and in 1997 F Bty 2RCHA, have represented Canada on AMF(L) exercises.

(Above) Lance-corporal of 2RCHA guarding his battery position, armed with the Diemaco 5.56mm C7A1 rifle; note subdued insignia of regiment, nationality and rank.

(Left) Serving in Bosnia under IFOR, one of the four M113A1 TUA armoured vehicles of 1RCR's anti-tank platoon; note twin TOW launcher turret. The Norwegians also use this vehicle, while Switzerland is mounting the Canadian turret on its MOWAG Piranhas.

(Above) F Bty's new 105mm LG1 MkII Light Gun, deployed under AMF(L) for the first time to Turkey for "Ardent Ground 97", can fire both in high trajectory as a howitzer and, as here, in flat trajectory against armour or bunkers. Its turntable platform allows fast traversing; with a complete crew of seven trained men it can fire up to 12 rounds per minute; and range with M1 HE at high trajectory is 11.5km - extending to 17.5km with HE BB ammunition (7 to 10.8 miles).

(Right) Cleaning guns after a day on the Turkish ranges. The Medium Logistics Vehicle Wheeled, a Canadian version of the M35A2, tows the gun and carries crew and ammunition.

United States

As the largest NATO partner the USA puts under AMF(L) command the following units:

1/508 Airborne Battalion Combat Team (ABCT)
D Battery, 319 Airborne Field Artillery Regt
Headquarters Company, 3COSCOM
Aviation Detachment, 6th Aviation Regt (SETAF)
A Company, 16 Engineer Bn
Platoon, B Co, 5/2 Air Defense Regt
Water Platoon, 240 Quartermaster Co
National Support Element

The smaller units are stationed in Germany, but the bulk of the US contingent is based at Vicenza in Italy, where they form the Southern European Task Force. SETAF is part of the US 82nd Airborne Division, and the 1/508th is the only airborne infantry unit stationed outside the USA.

In 1996 the 3rd Battalion (Airborne), 325th Infantry Regt was renamed **1st Battalion (Airborne), 508th Infantry Regiment**; since June 1996 it has carried the designation Airborne Battalion Combat Team. The battalion has an HQ and service company, a support company, and three equally structured rifle companies. Each rifle company has three 34-man platoons and a command section. Each of the platoon's three nine-strong rifle sections carries two 5.56mm M249 Squad Automatic Weapons (the US version of the Belgian Minimi), five 5.56mm M16A2 rifles, and two M16A2 with integral M203 40mm grenade launchers. The command section has two 7.62mm M60 machine guns, two M47 Dragon ATGWs, and a sniper team with the M21 rifle. Depending on the mission a large number of 84mm AT-4 light shoulder-fired anti-armour weapons can be issued to riflemen. Each company HQ element has two M224 60mm mortars.

The support company combines a mortar platoon with six M252 81mm tubes; two anti-tank platoons each with ten TOW mounted on Humvee vehicles; a field engineer platoon, an assault engineer platoon, and a reconnaissance platoon. The HQ and service company includes medical, signals, supply and maintenance platoons in addition to the command elements.

The artillery component since 1973 - **D Bty, 319 Airborne Field Arty Regt** - is also stationed at Vicenza. It fields six 105mm M119A1 Light Guns, very similar to the equivalent British model apart from a shorter barrel; and commands three FOO teams. The US Army also puts one platoon of **B Co, 5th Bn, 2nd Air Defense Regt** under AMF(L) command; stationed at Bamberg in Germany, it is equipped with 18 Avenger mobile AA rocket systems.

Also at Bamberg is **A Co, 16 Engineer Battalion**. Responsible for the whole range of engineer missions which may arise in the operational area, the unit has all necessary equipment for mine laying and mine clearance, as well as for earth-moving tasks such as digging anti-tank ditches or field fortifications. It often happens - as e.g. in eastern or southern Turkey - that the infrastructure of the deployment areas is insufficient to provide units of AMF(L) with drinking water, or that the roads and tracks are not practical march routes due to dilap-

This paratrooper sergeant serves with the mortar platoon of 1/508 ABCT, Southern Europe Task Force. The maroon beret, with regimental crest and colour backing, has been worn by 82nd Airborne Div. personnel at most times since 1973, though only officially authorised in 1981. Note SETAF's Lion of St Mark patch worn between the Airborne title and national flag on his left sleeve.

idated bridges or embankments. During exercises the US engineers have often reinforced bridges or rebuilt road surfaces, laid drainage systems or improved water pumping facilities, to the subsequent benefit of the local inhabitants. Altogether the engineer company's four platoons field four M48 AVLB armoured bridging vehicles, nine M113A2s, four M977 HEMTT 10-ton trucks, six M9 ACE armoured combat earth movers, four 5-ton trucks, four M99s and six HMMWVs.

(Above) 105mm light gun of D Bty, 319 Abn Fd Arty in travelling configuration. The versatile Humvees tow the guns, carry the battery's immediate use ammo, and transport the six-man crews and their equipment.

(Left) Gunners of D/319 prepare for a direct fire mission. The 105mm M119A1 differs from the British Light Gun in its shorter barrel, improved sight, brackets for a battery computer, M90 muzzle velocity measurement system, modified tie-down brackets, and use of nitrogen in the recoil system. Traverse is 360 degrees (at high speed) when using the platform, 11 degrees otherwise; elevation is from +70 to -5.5 degrees. Most crews add names to their gun barrels - e.g. "Mortal Combat", "Ugly Ducks", "Rejects", "Cheatin' Beth", etc.

(Left) Paratroopers of the 1/508th (note right shoulder patch) fight through a "FIBUA village" - a training site for fighting in built-up areas. They are heavily loaded with ALICE packs and personal equipment, and armed with the standard US Army M16A2 5.56mm rifle.

(Below) Photographed before the 1996 change of designation (note right shoulder patch of 82nd Abn.Div.), troopers of the 3/325th on radio watch enjoy a game of chess.

(Right) 1/508th ABCT machine gun crew manning the belt-fed 7.62mm M60. For the sake of its longer effective range than 5.56mm weapons (about 1,100m with bipod, or 1,800m on sustained fire tripod), two are still carried in the rifle platoon command section.

(Below) The M113A2 is used as the section vehicle within A Co, 16th Engineers; it can carry the personnel and all equipment necessary for carrying out light engineering tasks. Rucksacks and snowshoes can be seen among the concertina wire, etc., stowed outside this winter-camouflaged APC.

(Above) The engineers contribute powerfully to the "hearts and minds" aspect of the AMF(L) mission. Their work to improve local infrastructure - like this M578 ARV replacing a damaged bridge on a road destined to be a main supply route - lives on after the deterrence phase is completed.

(Right) Avenger of 5/2nd Air Defense Regt - a two-man, 3.9 ton Humvee mounting a turret with eight Stingers and an M3P machine gun; four spare rounds are carried, and a standard launcher for dismounted use. The mounted sensor pack includes CAI optical sight, Magnavox FLIR, DBA automatic video tracker and T1 laser range-finder. The turret can be operated from inside, or by remote control from up to 50m away.